诸子百家国风画传

Pictorial Biographies of Great Thinkers

老子画传

图/文 郭德福

译 秦悦

LAOZI

济南出版社

图书在版编目（CIP）数据

老子画传／郭德福著 .—— 济南：济南出版社，2015.8（诸子百家国风画传）
ISBN 978-7-5488-1755-0（2017.4 重印）

Ⅰ. ①老… Ⅱ. ①郭… Ⅲ. ①老子－传记－画册Ⅳ. ① B223.1-64

中国版本图书馆 CIP 数据核字 (2015) 第 209351 号

◆图、文／郭德福　　◆译／秦悦

◎ "原动力" 中国原创动漫出版扶持计划入选项目
◎ 上海市重大文艺创作项目由上海文化发展基金会资助
◎ 上海市文化 "走出去" 项目由上海市文化 "走出去" 专项扶持资金赞助

老子画传

出版发行	济南出版社
总 执 行	上海海派连环画中心
	上海城市动漫出版传媒有限公司
	济南出版有限责任公司
图书策划	刘 军　刘亚军
出版策划	崔 刚　朱孔宝
出版执行	张承军
责任编辑	李钰欣　张雪丽
特约编辑	刘蓉蓉　孙羽翎　余 阳　董广印
装帧设计	舒晓春　焦萍萍

印　　刷	山东海蓝印刷有限公司
开　　本	210×285　　1/16
印　　张	6.75
字　　数	105 千字
版　　次	2015 年 8 月第 1 版
印　　次	2017 年 4 月第 2 次印刷
标准书号	ISBN 978-7-5488-1755-0
定　　价	50.00 元

老子画传
LAOZI

前言

2014年3月，中国国家主席习近平在联合国教科文组织总部的演讲中指出：『中华文明经历了五千多年的历史变迁，但始终一脉相承，积淀着中华民族最深层的精神追求，代表着中华民族独特的精神标识，为中华民族生生不息、发展壮大提供了丰厚滋养。』中华传统文化是涓涓流水，润物无声，滋养了世代中国人的精神家园。在中华传统文化波澜壮阔的历史画卷中，诸子百家文化就是其中浓墨重彩的一页。

充满先贤智慧的诸子百家文化，是集中华传统文化、哲学、艺术于一体的文明宝藏：反对暴力，期盼人与人之间和睦相处、以礼相待，这是儒家思想的『仁』；平等博爱，止息不义战争，这是墨家思想的『兼爱非攻』；遵循自然、万物和谐，这是道家思想的『道法自然』；论兵却主张『不战而屈人之兵』，这是充满智慧光芒的兵家思想……诸子百家的思想，正包含着人们所努力构造的幸福世界中的重要基石。这是中华民族的财富，也是世界文明的重要组成部分。

近代以来，上海作为中华文明走向世界的一个重要窗口，担当着向世界展示中国文化华彩精粹的重要使命。建设充满活力的国际文化大都市，上海更需要放眼全球、放眼全国，以『海纳百川』的精神打造中华文化精品，推动中华文化走向世界。

这套由国务院新闻办公室支持，上海市政府新闻办公室发起，山东省政府新闻办公室、河南省政府新闻办公室协力出版的《诸子百家国风画传》丛书，化繁难为轻逸、化艰深为平易，充满了思想美、故事美、人性美、艺术美。它将诸子思想中的妙笔华章与国画家的水墨丹青巧妙结合，书香墨趣将诸子的音容笑貌、神采风骨生动地呈现在读者面前。它向世界打开了中华传统文化之门，同时也为中华文化拓展国际文化交流，进行了新的尝试和创新，提供了新的载体和通道。

诸子百家文化精神正如追逐理性、自由与美的古希腊人文精神一般，是人类共同的文化财富。希望诸位读者从这套书出发，分享故事，体验艺术，感悟哲理，开始一段美不胜收的中华传统文化探源之旅。

灿如云霞的中华文化让世人心向往之。

二〇一四年九月

Preface

In March of 2014, President Xi Jinping pointed out in his speech delivered in the headquarters of UNESCO, "Having gone through over 5000 years of vicissitudes, the Chinese civilization has always kept to its original root. Unique in representing China spiritually, it contains some most profound pursuits of the Chinese nation and provides it with abundant nourishment for existence and development." The Chinese traditional culture is just like trickling water irrigating and nurturing the spiritual realm of Chinese people. In the long and splendid picture of Chinese cultural history, the contributions of great thinkers are the most glorious chapter.

The wisdom and philosophies of these great thinkers crystallized culture, philosophy and art in our Chinese civilization: Confucian "benevolence", Mohist "universal love", Taoist "modeling itself after Nature" and the military teaching about "attaining victory in war without fighting" are still holding the stage. These fascinating thoughts constitute the cornerstones of an ideal world that Chinese people dream of having. These spiritual assets not only belong to Chinese people but also constitute an integral part of the world civilization.

As an important window in modern times, Shanghai has assumed a mission to demonstrate the brilliance of Chinese culture. To construct a dynamic international cultural metropolis and to promote Chinese culture to the world, Shanghai needs a mind so open to the entire country and entire world and a mind so tolerant as the vast ocean admitting hundreds of rivers.

The Pictorial Biographies of Great Thinkers supported by The State Council Information Office and Information Office of Shanghai Municipality is a close cooperation between Information Office of Shandong Provincial People's Government and Information Office of Henan Provincial People's Government. This series in Chinese painting style simplified the complicated history into simple stories，revealing the beauty of human nature as well as artistic creation. The ink painting presented vividly the personalities of great thinkers, attracting readers to explore their great thoughts and ideas. The pictorial biographies helped open the door of Chinese traditional culture to the world, and this attempt also provided a new carrier and channel for cultural exchange.

The brilliant Chinese culture is fascinating. Like the pursuit for reason, freedom and beauty in ancient Greek humanism, the legacy from these great thinkers is also the cultural assets shared by the whole humanity. It is hoped that readers can embark on a journey to explore traditional Chinese culture through reading these books.

September 2014

老子画传 LAOZI

编者的话

要想真正了解老子的思想，首先应该走进他的生活。画家郭德福沿着中国伟大的哲学家、思想家老子可考的生活足迹，先后游历了鹿邑、洛阳、函谷关、曲阜、周至等地，寻找老子遗留在世上的点点痕迹，经过多番实地采风，对老子的形象胸有成竹时，方才动笔编绘这本《老子画传》。

《老子画传》描绘了老子一生的历程，无论是总角小儿，或是弱冠青年，还是花甲老人……老子的形象都栩栩如生。为了呈现老子悟『道』过程中亦真亦幻、难以言说的文化风韵，郭德福在传统国画的基础上巧妙融入了当代绘画艺术的表现手法，让绘图更具艺术感染力。

尤为可贵的是，该书图文作者合一。郭德福对国学研究有着深厚的基础，在撰写文稿时，他吸收《史记》文体的历史真实、逻辑真实、艺术真实的风格，又融入生活真实，使全文生动易懂又不失韵味，画面鲜活，细节可考。文中用很多的篇幅描写老子的生活与交游，看似平淡，却微言大义，将老子『道法自然』的思想表现得淋漓尽致。

《老子画传》似一杯甘茗，读者只要静下心来细细品味，便能感悟到老子——这一参悟百态人生、乾坤宇宙奥秘的智者所遗留的真知灼见。

Editor's Note

It is advisable to get to know Laozi's life if you really want to understand his philosophical thinking. Guo Defu visited places such as Luyi, Luoyang, Hangu Pass, Qufu and Zhouzhi where Laozi is believed to have lived, and did not create this *Laozi* until he was confidently sure after his many field trips.

Laozi tries to represent as vividly as possible Laozi's entire life, from his childhood, to his adulthood, and to his advanced age. To demonstrate the indefinable revelation process Laozi got about Tao, Mr. Guo infused his traditional Chinese painting with the elements of contemporary artistic expression, enriching its artistic appeal.

What makes this book unusual is that Mr. Guo is both the artist and the author. Mr. Guo learned from a writing style that is unique to *Records of the Historian*, combining history and logic, art and reality, thus making his writing easy to understand without losing its charm. Laozi's daily social life is presented in a trivial but momentous way, illustrating fully Laozi's "the law of Tao is its being what it is".

Laozi is like a cup of tea lingering with its sweetness. All the readers need is a thirsty mind and they will understand the insightful observations left by Laozi, the sage revealing the secrets of life and the mysteries of the universe.

目录
Contents

◎老子母亲益寿氏教子图
Mother instructing little Li Er

　　大约在公元前 571 年，老子出生在春秋时期陈国　　寿氏为其取名李耳（字聃）。
的苦县（今河南省鹿邑县）。老子的父亲李乾、母亲益

天下万物生于有，有生于无。（《老子》第四十章）

Laozi, born in around 571B.C., was a native of Hu County (present-day Luyi County in Henan Province) of the State of Chen during the Spring and Autumn Period (770—476 B.C.). His parents named him Li Er (known in China as Lao Dan).

◎李耳牧牛图

Li Er pasturing the cattle

　　由于家境清贫，童年时李耳做过牧牛童。聪明的　　四季景物的变化，琢磨着大自然的奥秘。
李耳一边放牧，一边望天、望水、望树、望云，观察着

道生一，一生二，二生三，三生万物。（《老子》第四十二章）

Born into a poor family, Li Er worked as a cowherd when he was a child. He was a very sensitive and observant child. Li Er was looking far into the sky, deep into the water, and gazing at trees and clouds while the cattle were grazing in the field. He kept track of the changes of seasons, pondering the mysteries of nature.

◎乡童问树图

Children arguing about a tree

　　有一天，李耳在放牛途中，遇见一群小孩围着一棵大树争论不休。孩子们看见李耳，急忙拉他来做裁判，原来孩子们正在为这棵大树的品种而争论。

天之道，利而不害；圣人之道，为而不争。（《老子》第八十一章）

One day, Li Er saw a group of children standing around a tree and arguing. When they saw Li Er, they eagerly asked him to judge who was right about the tree.

◎李耳悟树图
Li Er giving an answer about the tree

李耳围着树转了一圈，也被难住了：这棵树从东面看像槐树，从西面看像楝树。它到底是棵什么树呢？

李耳一边观察一边思索，终于发现原来是一棵槐树苗与一棵楝树苗长在了一起，天长日久变成了一棵树。

天下有始，以为天下母。（《老子》第五十二章）

Li Er walked around the tree, but he was also unable to tell. This tree looked like a Chinese scholartree if looked from the east, but a chinaberry if looked from the west. What on earth was this tree? Li Er observed it carefully and thought for a while, finally he told others that the tree was actually not one tree but a sapling of Chinese scholartree and a chinaberry seedling, which had grown into a tree after a considerable period of time.

◎李耳拜师图

Li Er having a master

　　李耳说出自己的发现，并将这棵树命名为"合欢树"。李耳的一番话，被在此隐居的学者商容听到。商容见李耳颖悟绝伦又善于思考，便主动提出教李耳识字读书。

知人者智，自知者明。（《老子》第三十三章）

Li Er told them what he thought, and named the tree "hehuan". Shang Rong, a scholar in his seclusion here, overheard what Li Er had said. Impressed by his observation and cleverness, Shang Rong offered to teach him read and write.

◎李耳求学图
Li Er pursuing his studies

　　李耳随商容学习数年后，心智大开，他学会了将生活中的感受、对自然的感悟与所学文化知识融会贯通，举一反三。商容赞其日后必成大器，建议李耳远赴周都洛邑（今河南省洛阳市）至友人常枞处深造，并资助他远行。

有之以为利，无之以为用。（《老子》第十一章）

Li Er had made a remarkable mental breakthrough after learning under his master Shang Rong for years. Once a conscious breakthrough was made, Li Er was able to make a second, beginning his life-long perspective and collection about nature and life. Shang Rong thought highly of Li Er, believing him would make great achievements in the future. Shang Rong suggested Li Er should go to Luoyi (present-day Luoyang in Henan Province), the capital of Zhou to further his study with the help of Chang Cong, and funded his trip there.

◎李耳辞师远行图
Li Er bidding farewell to his master

　　临别时，李耳再次请求商容教诲。商容想了一下，便张开嘴，问李耳看到了什么。李耳说："您坚硬的牙齿没有了，但柔软的舌头还在。"商容说："见舌而知守柔，这就是我要告诉你的。"李耳记住了老师的话，洒泪拜别老师，踏上了赴周都洛邑之路。

天下之至柔，驰骋天下之至坚。（《老子》第四十三章）

Upon leaving, Li Er asked his master again for advice. Shang Rong opened his mouth and then asked Li Er what he had seen. "You have no strong teeth, but your soft tongue is still there." "That's what I want to tell you: keep soft to be strong." Li Er bore this in mind and said goodbye to his master in tears, and then embarked on his way to Luoyi.

◎李耳悟龙图

Li Er pondering the ancient dragon culture

　　李耳栉风沐雨地赶路，但每临古文化遗址，他都要仔细考察一番。在太昊陵（"太昊"是后世对伏羲的赞词）遗址，李耳思接远古，有感于伏羲创造了"龙"的形象，而龙最终成为中华民族的图腾。在晨雾缭绕的旷野中，李耳陷入对龙文化的思索中。

譬道之在天下，犹川谷之于江海。（《老子》第三十二章）

Li Er hurried on with his journey, rain or shine. Nonetheless, he slowed down in front of the historical relics on his way. On the historical site of Taihao Mausoleum (later generations addressed Fuxi as Taihao), Li Er thought more deeply about the ancient past, and wondered how Fuxi, the legendary Chinese ruler who taught people how to fish, hunt, and raise livestock had created the image of dragon, and how the dragon had become the totem of Chinese people. In the morning mist, Li Er sank into deep thought about the dragon culture in the wilderness.

◎李耳野炊舍饭图

Li Er sharing the rice with a beggar

　　一天雨后，李耳正在燃篝火煮饭，一个逃荒的乞丐前来乞讨，李耳说："饭还没熟，要不你等一下。"乞丐一听饭没熟就转身离去了。李耳等饭煮熟后，追上乞丐把饭送给他吃。乞丐十分感动，连说："你真是个大善之人！"随后他取出一堆散乱的简牍送给了李耳。

天道无亲，常与善人。（《老子》第七十九章）

Li Er was cooking over a bonfire after a rain when a beggar walked up and asked for some rice. Li Er said, "It is not done yet. Do you mind waiting for a while?" Hearing this, the beggar simply walked away. When the rice was cooked, Li Er went after him and offered him the food. The beggar was deeply touched and said, "You are so very kind!" Then he took out a pile of bamboo slips and gave them to Li Er.

◎李耳旅途悟经图

Li Er thinking about Tao

　　乞丐说："这些简牍，是同行的一位逃荒老者临终所赠。若是当柴烧了太可惜，还是送给你这位好心的读书人吧。"李耳细读后发现这是楚国名士老莱子所著的部分文章，如获至宝。从此，他昼读夜思，感悟到"反者道之动"——天道的本性是变动，变动的本质在于相反事物间的相互作用与转化。这一感悟，奠定了李耳认识事物的基础，也使李耳对事物本质的认识有了一个新跨越。

反者道之动；弱者道之用。（《老子》第四十章）

The beggar said, "An old dying man who fled from famine bequeathed these bamboo slips to me. It's a great shame if burned as firewood. You are such a warm-hearted and book-loving man, and I might just as well give them to you." After he perused them, Li Er found that some chapters were written by Lao Laizi, a famous thinker of the State of Chu, and he was overjoyed to have them. He read day and night, and came to the realization that the universe was on the constant change, and the nature of change lay in the interaction and interchange between contrary objects. The understanding about objects established his outlook about the world and shed new light on his perspectives about the nature of things.

◎常枞赏文图
Chang Cong appreciating Li Er's writing

挫其锐，解其纷，和其光，同其尘。（《老子》第四章）

　　长途跋涉月余，李耳终于来到洛邑。此地街市繁华，热闹非常。李耳不及细看，直奔老师推荐的友人常枞的住处。常枞是当朝史官，负责观测天文。他见李耳才学过人，写得一手好文章，满心欢喜，便有计划地把李耳引荐给洛邑各界名士，使李耳眼界大开。

　　Li Er finally arrived in Luoyi after months' trek. Although Luoyi was a hustling and bustling city, Li Er paid no notice to it, and went straight to where Chang Cong lived. As a historiographer, Chang Cong was in charge of astronomical observation. He highly appreciated Li Er for his talent and writing; therefore, Chang Cong designedly recommended Li Er to the academic circle in Luoyi. Thus meeting the famous scholars broadened Li Er's horizon.

◎李耳守藏室抄经图

Li Er copying classics in the library

　　李耳求知若渴，饱读经典，天文、地理无所不学，文物、典章无所不习，所以学问突飞猛进。常枞便引荐他入朝为官。公元前551年，年轻的李耳被周王室选为守藏室官吏。守藏室收藏典籍图书之多可谓汗牛充栋，李耳如鱼得水，阅览了所有藏书。李耳分类整理了守藏室繁杂的典籍图书，并誊写了一些珍贵的史料。在李耳的努力下，守藏室面貌一新。

人之所畏，不可不畏。（《老子》第二十章）

Li Er studied everything, including astronomy, geography, classic literature, rituals and rites, and he made rapid progress in every aspect. Chang Cong recommended him to take a post in the official career. In 551 B.C., the young Li Er was appointed as a librarian of the royal court. There were an abundance of books in the library, and Li Er enjoyed reading all the books as ducks enjoy water. Li Er organized all the books into different categories, and he went all the troubles to write down extra copies for some important historical documents. The library took on a completely new look due to his hard work.

◎李耳携子瀍河漫步图
Li Er walking with Li Zong

　　做了守藏室官吏的李耳，有了固定的收入后，便　　李耳常带李宗到瀍河岸边沙滩上漫步玩耍，引导儿子
在洛邑瀍河边安了家，娶妻生子。初为人父的李耳，为　　观察自然、热爱自然。
其子取名李宗。小李宗在父母的关爱下一天天长大。

大方无隅；大器晚成；大音希声；大象无形；道隐无名。（《老子》第四十一章）

As a librarian, Li Er got a regular income. He settled down in Luoyi, and then got married and became a father. He named his son Li Zong. Li Zong grew up under the care of his parents.

Li Er and Li Zong often strolled along the beach of the Chanhe River, having fun there. By observing nature, Li Er taught his son to follow the way of nature and love nature.

◎李耳夫妻植赏牡丹图

The couple admiring peonies

　　李耳与妻子都喜爱牡丹花。妻子外出时，见一人大夸其所卖的牡丹根，便买下一棵。凑巧李耳也在路上遇到一位卖牡丹根的人。李耳见此人不善言辞，便买了一棵牡丹根。两棵牡丹长大后，李耳买的牡丹花开艳美，妻子买的牡丹却只长叶、不开花，细看原来它是一棵不值钱的野蓁树。李耳悟道："信言不美，美言不信。"

信言不美，美言不信。（《老子》第八十一章）

Both Li Er and his wife loved peony flowers. Li Er's wife bought a peony root when a seller boasted how good it was. Li Er also met a man sell peony root. The man was not good at crying out, but Li Er still bought one from him. The two peonies grew bigger. The one Li Er bought was in full blooming, while the one his wife bought only came into leaves —it turned out to be a wild caltrop. Li Er came to see the point, "Sincere words are not fine; fine words are not sincere."

◎益寿氏望孙学步图
Grandma and toddler

知其雄，守其雌，为天下谿。（《老子》第二十八章）

有了家室的李耳亲自回鹿邑接母亲来洛邑同住。母亲益寿氏见到可爱的孙子李宗，自然十分高兴，尽享天伦之乐。可是时间长了，母亲不免思念家乡。每当

这时，李耳就与母亲回忆自己童年顽皮的样子，时而做出童年憨态，引得母亲开怀大笑。

Li Er went back to his hometown Luyi to visit his mother, inviting her to stay with his family in Luoyi. Mother was very excited to see her lovely grandson and enjoyed the family

reunion for a while. But Mother soon felt homesick. Seeing this, Li Er talked about good old times and fond memories about his own childhood with naivety, Mother couldn't help laughing.

◎李耳携子瀍河戏水图

Li Er and Li Zong having fun in the Chanhe River

　　李耳很重视对李宗的教育。在瀍河岸边，他向儿子讲解"上善若水"的道理。在教会儿子游泳后，他告诫儿子在尽享浮水之乐时，也要知晓水亦淹人的潜在危险。他将追求合于天道、顺乎自然、"往而不害，安平泰"的生活理念传授给李宗。

上善若水。水善利万物而不争，处众人之所恶，故几于道。（《老子》第八章）

Li Er attached importance to his son's education. On the bank of the Chanhe River, he explained the meaning of "The greatest virtue is like water, nourishing everything without competing for repute". He taught his son how to swim, telling his son to enjoy floating on the water, but mean while know the potential danger of being drowned. He instilled into his son the concept that one's pursuit should be in compliance with Tao. In this case, "people resorting to him will not receive hurt, but rest, peace, and the feeling of ease."

◎老子柱下记事图
Laozi recording events by the pillar

圣人后其身而身先；外其身而身存。（《老子》第七章）

　　数年后，李耳又升为守藏室史（相当于现在的国家档案馆和图书馆馆长），负责记载史事、掌管史籍和撰写史书等事务。随着学识、官位的提高，李耳声名远扬，人们就尊称他为"老子""老聃"。老子还负责在朝廷上做记录，记载史事。周天子特旨恩准，在朝堂上树立一根柱子，让老子可以倚柱记事，于是后人便把守藏室史称为"柱下史"。在数十年的记史过程中，老子对国势兴衰、决策正误，都有了真切的感悟与思索。他最终将这些感悟写入《老子》。

　　Years later, Li Er was promoted to a higher post (a post is similar to the director of National Archives and National Library). He was in charge of recording historical happenings, filing archives and writing historical records. As his learning and post enhanced, his reputation spread afar, and he was called respectfully "Laozi" or "Laodan". Laozi was also in charge of recording what happened in the royal court. The Emperor of Zhou specifically had a pillar erected in the royal hall so that Laozi could take notes, standing against the pillar. That's why Laozi is also called "historiographer by the pillar".Laozi spent over ten years recording the ups and downs of a country, decision-making of the king, which gave him real feelings and thoughts. Finally, he put his thoughts into *Laozi*.

◎老子民间采风图

Laozi collecting folk songs

除了记录史事、整理典籍文献外，老子还经常带着儿子李宗造访各地，收集民歌、民谣和传说。这些具有浓郁生活气息、神秘而浪漫的民间抒情诗歌，直接影响了他日后著述《老子》的语言风格。

天下难事，必作于易；天下大事，必作于细。（《老子》第六十三章）

Apart from recording historical events, classifying archives, Laozi often took his son with him to different places to collect folk songs, ballads and legends. Having been infused with rich flavor of life, mystery and romance, these lyric poetries directly influenced his writing of *Laozi*.

◎老子直言图
Laozi stating candidly

宠辱若惊，贵大患若身。（《老子》第十三章）

　　周王室日渐衰微，政权被诸公卿把握。他们结党营私，争权夺利。周王室的甘氏一族由甘简公掌权，他与甘成公、甘景公的族人不和，把国政搞得乌烟瘴气。

老子恪守职责，如实记载国事。甘简公因此大怒，免去了老子守藏室史之职。

　　The Zhou Dynasty was declining. The power was controlled by different dukes and ministers. They formed cliques and fought for their own interests. The royal family was controlled by the Gan clan. Duke Jian of Gan was in control of the power, but he was in discord with his clansmen Duke Cheng and Duke Jing. Their internal strife threw the country into chaos and confusion. Because Laozi recorded faithfully what had happened, Duke Jian flew into rage and removed Laozi from his office.

◎南荣趎拜师求学图

Nanrong Chu requesting to learn under Laozi

　　罢官后的老子，与家人回到故乡鹿邑。他在鹿邑修建学舍，授徒讲学。楚国有位叫南荣趎的青年，走了七天七夜，来向老子求学。老子一见面就问道："子何与人偕来之众也？"明明南荣趎独自而来，而老子却问他为什么带着那么多的人来。其实此"众"字，是指众多的世俗杂念。由此可见老子灵活的教育方法——他"当头棒喝"，目的是让南荣趎进行深入思考，然后再开导其心。

为学日益，为道日损。（《老子》第四十八章）

After he was dismissed, Laozi went back to his hometown Luyi and ran a school there. Nanrong Chu, a young man from the State of Chu, walked for seven days and nights to visit Laozi. Seeing him, Laozi asked, "Why do you come with so many persons?" Nanrong Chu came alone, but Laozi asked why he came with so many persons. "Many persons" here means many worldly distractions. Laozi was very flexible with his approach—his timely warning directed Nanrong Chu to think deeply first by himself, and then Laozi would enlighten him.

◎ 老子讲学图

The teaching style of Laozi

　　当时的普通话——雅言，是以周都洛邑的语音为基础的。老子长期生活在洛邑，能说一口流利的雅言，面对操着不同方言的学生，老子用雅言讲学，通过讲学、授徒让雅言走入民间。老子还率先把西周兴起的简牍文化引入教学，用毛笔在竹简上书写当时通用的大篆。老子为推动雅言、简牍、大篆在教学中的使用，做出了不可磨灭的贡献。

见素抱朴，少私寡欲。（《老子》第十九章）

The common speech of the Chinese language—*yayan* spoken at that time had the pronunciation of the capital of Zhou, Luoyi dialect as its basis. As Laozi lived there long enough to be able to speak fluent *yayan*, he lectured in *yayan* to disciples from different states. Through lecturing and teaching, *yayan* initiated by Laozi and his disciples eventually made its way into the general vernacular. Laozi also introduced bamboo slips into teaching, writing Chinese characters of large seal script, which was an ancient style of calligraphy on the bamboo slips with a writing brush. Laozi made remarkable contribution to popularizing in teaching the common speech of the Chinese language then, the using of bamboo slips and the Chinese writing of large seal script.

◎老子与弟子赏月图
Laozi admiring the moon with his disciples

　　中秋之夜，老子与弟子们登高赏月。老子的学生有杨朱、文子、庚桑楚、南郭子綦等。其中杨朱因说出"人人不损一毫，人人不利天下，天下治矣"而闻名；文子后来成为范蠡的老师，而范蠡是一位全面实践老子思想的名人；南郭子綦后来则为庄子的老师，庄子亦是将道家学说发扬光大的主要人物。

　　老子回到鹿邑后不久，母亲益寿氏过世了，于是老子安葬了母亲（益寿氏墓在今鹿邑县太清宫镇）。

杨朱，先秦哲学家，战国时期魏国人，道家杨朱学派的创始人。

During the night of Mid-Autumn Festival, Laozi and his disciples climbed up to the top of a mountain to admire the bright full moon. Yang Zhu, Wenzi, Gensang Chu and Nanguo Ziqi were Laozi's disciples. Yang Zhu was known for what he said "If everyone does not have to sacrifice their own interests, then the world is in good order". Wenzi was Fan Li's master, and Fan Li was a famous person who comprehensively implemented Laozi's idea. Nanguo Ziqi was Zhuangzi's master, and Zhuangzi carried on Laozi's philosophy.

Soon after Laozi went back to Luyi, his mother passed away. Subsequently Laozi buried his mother (his mother's tomb is in Taiqing Palace Town in Luyi County).

◎老子、孔子送葬遇日食图
Solar eclipse on a funeral service

物壮则老，是谓不道，不道早已。（《老子》第三十章）

数年后，老子带着儿子李宗应邀赴鲁国考察周礼。有一友人不幸去世，老子为其安排丧事，年轻的孔子也参加了。出葬途中，忽遇日食，老子果断令送葬队伍停止前进，待日食过后再行。送葬归来，孔子向老子请教其中道理。老子告诉孔子："大夫出访时都是日出而行，日落而歇，送葬也应如此。黑夜行路者，只有罪犯。日食如同黑夜，所以我让送葬队伍停下来，等日食过后，天亮再走。"

Years later, Laozi took his son Li Zong with him to the State of Lu to observe and study the rites and rituals of the Zhou Dynasty. One of Laozi's friends passed away, and Laozi arranged the funeral. The young Confucius attended the mourning. On their way to the graveyard, a solar eclipse occurred. Laozi immediately stopped the funeral procession, and started again only after the solar eclipse was gone. Confucius asked Laozi for the reason. Laozi explained, "Officials start their traveling when the sun rises, and stops when the sun sets. The same is also true for the funeral procession. Only criminals set off at night. When the solar eclipse occurs, it is as dark as night. So I asked the procession to stop till the eclipse was gone and it was bright again."

◎老子与李宗话别图

Laozi saying parting words to Li Zong

　　老子的儿子李宗是个志向远大的青年，他决定远游列国，寻找实现人生理想的机遇。行前老子与儿子交流心声，将"道常无为而无不为""以道佐人主者，不以兵强天下"等治国理念、管理方法、统兵策略，都做了详细讲解。李宗后来成为魏国名将，他善于将父亲的理论应用于社会实践，解决实际问题。

道生之，德畜之，物形之，势成之。（《老子》第五十一章）

Li Zong was a young ambitious man. He decided to travel far to see the world. Laozi had a heart-to-heart conversation with his son, discussing at length his concepts about governing a country, management approaches and military strategies. Ideas such as "Tao (or the way) acts through non-action" "He who assists the emperor with the principle of Tao will not conquer the world by force of arms" took roots in Li Zong's mind. When Li Zong later became a famous general in the State of Wei, he applied what he had been taught to resolve social conflicts.

◎老子复职图

Laozi being restored to his former post

　　公元前530年，周王室甘简公的弟弟甘悼公企图
消灭甘成公、甘景公这两支力量，结果失败了。老子曾
因得罪甘简公而被罢官，甘成公、甘景公视老子为甘

简公的对立面，将老子官复原职，于是老子又回到周
都洛邑。

祸兮，福之所倚；福兮，祸之所伏。（《老子》第五十八章）

In 530 B.C., Duke Dao of Gan, the younger brother of Duke Jian, failed to wipe out Duke Cheng and Duke Jing. Having been dismissed for offending Duke Jian, Laozi was regarded as Duke Jian's opponent by Duke Cheng and Duke Jing, and then he was restored to his former post. Therefore, Laozi went back to Luoyi, the capital of Zhou.

◎ 老子爱孙图
Laozi caring for his grandson

　　文子来洛邑看望老子，一进门，便见老子怀里抱着熟睡中的孙儿李注。老子深情地注视着孙子，对文子说："你看婴儿常常啼哭，喉咙却不会嘶哑，这是因为婴儿的啼哭自然又和谐；婴儿的筋骨柔弱，但小拳头整天握得很紧，这正是婴儿的常态啊。婴儿天真素朴，顺任自然。我想，这就是我们为人应该关注的修养境界吧。"

专气致柔，能如婴儿乎？（《老子》第十章）

Wenzi, a disciple of Laozi, came to Luoyi to visit him. Laozi was holding his sleeping grandson Li Zhu in his arms, while looking at him benignly. Laozi said to Wenzi, "The babies often cry, but their voice will not hoarse. That's because their way of producing sound is natural. Although the babies have their soft bodies, they hold their fists tight, and they do so just as a matter of course. Babies take in things as what they are and will not go against nature. In my view, this is supposed to be the extent reached that we had better conduct ourselves."

◎孔子、老子相见图（一）
Confucius meeting with Laozi（1）

执大象，天下往。往而不害，安平泰。（《老子》第三十五章）

公元前 518 年，34 岁的孔子在鲁昭公的资助下，千里迢迢到洛邑向老子求学。途经黄河时，孔子射下一只大雁，作为送给老子的见面礼，老子闻讯亲自出城相迎。

In 518 B. C., funded by Duke Zhao of Lu, the 34-year-old Confucius had a trip to Luoyi. He traveled all the way to visit Laozi. Confucius shot a wild goose as a gift for Laozi when crossing the Yellow River. Laozi went out of the city to meet Confucius.

◎孔子、老子相见图（二）
Confucius meeting with Laozi（2）

　　老子先带孔子阅读馆藏经典。孔子看了《商颂》《周颂》及上古文献三千余篇，还将一些重点文献誊写下来，为后来编撰《春秋》打下了基础。老子又邀请孔子到家中做客，并将家人介绍给孔子。老子与孔子闲聊时，提及自己人生第一位老师是哑巴，孔子好奇，老子大笑道："哑巴老师是一棵树。"于是老子便将童年辨识合欢树的趣事告诉孔子。孔子听后沉思良久，从中悟出格物致知的道理，即透过事物表象来探知其内在的联系与本质。

知者不言，言者不知。（《老子》第五十六章）

Confucius browsed the classics in the library. He read *The Songs of Shang*, *The Songs of Zhou* and other more than three thousand historical documents, and took down some important literature, which contributed a lot to his writing of *The Spring and Autumn Annals*. Laozi entertained Confucius in his home, and introduced his family members to Confucius. In their chatting, Laozi told Confucius that his first teacher was a mute, and Confucius was surprised to learn that. Laozi laughed and told him, "My mute teacher was a tree." Then Laozi told Confucius how he decided the tree was actually not one but two. Confucius ruminated over the interesting story and learned that one could only obtain knowledge by making investigations to see through the surface of things and explore their internal connections.

◎老子、孔子论"无为而治"图
Laozi and Confucius on governing

　　一日，孔子向老子表达了希望争取机会从政、推行仁政的济世理念。老子向孔子介绍了"无为而无不为"，顺应事物自身发展的规律，借势而为，便会治理好各类政务的施政方案。老子又详谈了"无为"的具体操作细节，及对实施"无为"者必须具备仁德品格的要求。接着，老子又回顾家乡陈国的先祖即是以"无为"治国闻名的舜。孔子听后感悟道："无为而治者，其舜也与！"

无为而无不为。（《老子》第四十八章）

Confucius told Laozi his political pursuit of benevolence. Laozi shared with Confucius his concept of governing. That is, governing everything without seeming to be doing it, just let it be. Laozi discussed in detail how to govern without doing anything that goes against nature, and the virtues required of him who wanted to adopt the approach. Laozi then cited the example of Shun, a well-respected emperor known for his "governing without seeming to be doing it" in the State of Chen, his hometown. Confucius said in admiration, "No one is better than Shun."

◎老子晒发图
A loose-haired Laozi

　　一日，孔子去拜访老子，刚进院门，便看到刚洗过头发的老子正在牡丹花丛旁晒发，神态虚静如槁木。须发飘飘的老子似进入"天人合一""物我两忘"的境地，孔子遂向老子请教如何能达到虚静之境。老子说："致虚极，守静笃。万物并作，吾以观复。"意思是说，清静无欲是正确深入认识事物的最佳状态。

致虚极，守静笃。万物并作，吾以观复。（《老子》第十六章）

One day, Confucius visited Laozi. When he stepped into the courtyard, he saw Laozi sitting beside peonies, letting his hair loose and drying it under the sun. A dreamy, faraway and yet quiet look came over Laozi's face. He looked like a withered tree. The grey-haired Laozi seemed to be lost into a placid inner state. Confucius then asked Laozi how to get into the state of dreamy, faraway and yet placid communion between oneself and the nature. Laozi said, "The stillness and emptiness should be brought to the utmost degree, and you can see all things alike go through from static to dynamic state, in a circular way." That is to say, withstanding the temptation of selfish desire the man can gain an in-depth understanding of the nature of things.

◎老子、孔子论"荆人失弓"图

A debate on the loss of a bow

　　一日，老子、文子与孔子在谈话中说起"荆人失弓"的故事。荆人丢了弓而不去寻找，却说："荆人遗之，荆人得之，又何索焉？"孔子听后，认为应去掉"荆"字，爱所有的人；老子则进一步要求去掉"人"字，泛爱万物，视万物与人为一体。

老子孔子论
荆人失弓图

郭德福 童莘题
特平二年 有子
燿福

天地不仁，以万物为刍狗；圣人不仁，以百姓为刍狗。（《老子》第五章）

One day, Laozi, Wenzi and Confucius talked about a man of Jing (the State of Chu) lost his bow in local area. He lost his bow and decided not to look for it. He said, "A man of Jing lost his bow in his own place, and another man of Jing will get it. Why bother to look for it?" Confucius' reaction to the story was that the word "Jing" should be deleted to show the man's love for all the human beings, while Laozi thought that the word "man" should also be deleted to show the man's universal love for everything.

◎老子为孙打枣图
Laozi picking jujubes for his grandson

　　一日，孔子又去拜访老子，他推门进院，看见老子正在为孙儿李注打枣。孔子被眼前天伦之乐的情景所打动，亦去帮助打枣。老子告诉孔子，此枣树是母亲益寿氏当年特意从家乡苦县带来的，如今硕果累累，而思母之心愈重，枣子也更加显得甜脆。孔子听罢，笑道："真巧，我在曲阜阙里家院中，也有一棵母亲当年手植的枣树，每当枣子成熟时，我都会精心挑选一些，祭母时上供使用。"

人之生也柔弱，其死也坚强。（《老子》第七十六章）

One day, Laozi was beating the jujubes off the tree with a stick and his grandson Li Zhu was eating jujubes when Confucius visited him. Confucius was so attracted to such a loving scene that he immediately joined them. Laozi told Confucius the jujube tree was once a seedling his mother specifically gave him from his hometown. The tree was now laden with countless jujubes. His recalling with deep feeling of his mother grew stronger, the jujubes tasted sweeter. Confucius smiled and said, "It so happens that there is also a jujube tree my mother planted in my courtyard in Qufu. When the jujubes are ripe, I would always handpick some and give my mother as offerings."

◎老子、孔子瀍河泛舟图

Loazi and Confucius boating on the Chanhe River

　　老子与孔子乘舟从瀍河旁的老子家宅到周都守藏室。在船上，老子向孔子讲述了他对水的感悟。他们望着瀍河边怒放的荷花，孔子对荷花出淤泥而不染的品质十分赞赏。老子说："水善于滋润万物却不与万物相争，心甘情愿地处于众人都不喜欢的低洼之处，所以最接近于道。"

江海之所以能为百谷王者，以其善下之，故能为百谷王。（《老子》第六十六章）

Laozi and Confucius took a boat from Laozi's place to the Library of Zhou. Laozi shared his understanding about water. Seeing the full-blooming lotus flowers, which were intact of the muddy water, Confucius was impressed by their purity. Then Laozi said, "Whether the person or thing that has the highest excellence is just like water nurturing and nourishing everything without competing. They stay at the lowest place which most others dislike. So this kind of person or thing is very close to Tao."

◎老子、孔子邙山畅谈图

Laozi and Confucius talking on Mangshan Mountain

老子引领孔子参观郊外天子祭天、祭地的场所,"观先王之遗制,考礼乐之所极"。途中孔子驾车,老子乘车,二人迎风而行。老子、孔子都爱登山望水,归来时他们登上洛邑北郊的邙山翠云峰,置身山顶,极目远眺,无限风光尽收眼底。老子畅谈自己"小国寡民"的政治理念。他追求的小国寡民之世,是风淳太平之世,在这小天地里,人们生活安定,不动干戈。孔子也表达了推行仁政、天下为公的美好愿望。

圣人常无心，以百姓心为心。（《老子》第四十九章）

Laozi took Confucius to the temples for heaven and earth worship. Confucius studied the systems the late emperors practiced, and examined the heights that rituals and rites can reach. They rode a carriage against the wind. Both of them enjoyed mountains and rivers. On the return of their journey, they climbed up to the top of Mangshan Mountain where beautiful sceneries in the distance came in sight. Laozi talked about his political idea of a peaceful small country with a small population. What he pursued was people there could live a stable life without being afflicted by wars. Confucius also expressed his political ideals of benevolence and "the world should be all people's world".

◎老子、孔子、苌弘论乐图
Laozi, Confucius and Chang Hong appreciating music

老子又引孔子拜访了周都乐师苌弘，三人一起探讨"乐"的文化渊源，留下了关于大型舞乐《大武》的经典论述。孔子在洛邑问礼之行，历时近一年，几乎每天都有新发现、新思考。孔子与老子建立了深厚的友谊，分别时，老子送孔子至黄河之滨。

有无相生，难易相成，长短相形，高下相盈，音声相和，前后相随。（《老子》第二章）

Laozi introduced Confucius to Chang Hong, the music master of Zhou. They had a discussion about the cultural origin of music and the music and dance of *Great Wu*. Confucius studied in Luoyi for almost one year, and had new ideas and thoughts every day. Confucius and Laozi established a profound friendship. When Confucius left for home, Laozi saw him off to the bank of the Yellow River.

◎孔子、老子黄河话别图
Confucius saying goodbye to Laozi

　　望着浩浩荡荡的黄河，老子动情地说："我听说富贵之人用财物送人，仁义之人用言语送人。我非富贵之人，愧用仁人的名义，用言语来送你。"孔子认真听完老子的临别赠言，与老子施礼而别。归途中，孔子在学生面前对老子称赞不已，说老子像龙一样高深莫测。

大丈夫处其厚，不居其薄；处其实，不居其华。（《老子》第三十八章）

Looking at the rushing Yellow River, Laozi said excitedly to Confucius, "I was told that rich people give friends expensive gifts, and benevolent people share words with his friends. I'm not rich. But let me be a benevolent person and offer you some advice." Confucius listened with respect to his parting words, and bowed a goodbye to him. On his way back, Confucius told his disciples that Laozi was as mysterious as a dragon.

◎老子临水抒怀图

Laozi expressing emotion by the water

　　公元前 518 年，周王室发生内乱，王子朝争夺王位失败，带着周王室的典籍逃往楚国。老子蒙受失职之责，再次被罢免了官职。于是，老子在离开周都去宋国沛泽的途中，临水抒怀："澹兮，其若海；飂兮，若无止。"意思是，我的心那样辽阔，就像大海无边无际；思绪就像疾风劲吹，飘扬万里没有尽头。老子的与众不同体现在他看重道的滋养。

道常无为而无不为。（《老子》第三十七章）

In 518 B.C., there was an internal strife in the royal family. The prince failed in competing for the crown, and fled to the State of Chu with some royal documents. Laozi was liable for negligence, and was removed from office again. Laozi had to leave the capital of Zhou for Peize in the State of Song. On his way, Laozi lamented by the water, "My heart is as vast as a sea and as erratic as wind." What made Laozi special is Tao can help with his self-cultivation.

◎老子隐居沛泽图
Laozi living in seclusion in Peize

　　南荣趎专程来沛泽看望老子。他讲述了自己在求学问道之路上的新困惑。老子思索片刻，说："注重修养的人，才能保持较高的修养境界，人们就会亲近他，上天也会帮助他。学习的人，学到不能再学的地步（而停下）；行路的人，走到不能再走的境地（而停下）；辩论的人，辩论到无可争辩的程度（而停下）。知道在不能再有所知的地方停下，那就是到了极限了。如果不是这样，那么上天就会让他败亡。"南荣趎听后，茅塞顿开，在沛泽住了几日后，便辞师远游去了。

不出户，知天下；不窥牖，见天道。（《老子》第四十七章）

Nanrong Chu, a disciple of Laozi came to Peize to visit him. Nanrong Chu told Laozi that he found it was hard to made breakthrough in his academic studies. Laozi thought for a while and said, "He who attaches great importance to cultivation will make progress and will be helped along. To study is to learn that is not available to us; to travel is to go to places that are not accessible to us; to distinguish is to tell apart the undistinguishable. If you stay in the state of the unknown, you will reach the extreme of knowing." Nanrong Chu was enlightened and went on his journey of seeking knowledge after he stayed in Peize for a few days.

望駒圖

中華民族歷來有詩禮傳家之文明家風之明。重視子女之教育，以致家庭和諧，社會之明。庭和諧，社會之樂。明王倫之樂，孫滿堂，為人生之追求。余繪斯圖，冀以述此中愛意，以記之也。

◎老子携孙望驹图
Laozi and his grandson feeding a pony

知足不辱，知止不殆，可以长久。（《老子》第四十四章）

老子在沛泽见到了小孙子李同，对他关爱有加，除教他读书识字外，还时常带他与村童一道喂马饲牛、打枣摘瓜，于隐居生活中尽享天伦之乐。李同后来成为赵国的大将军。

Laozi spent sometime with his another grandson Li Tong in Peize. Laozi loved Li Tong very much. He taught him to read and took him to the farm to feed horses, pick jujubes and melons. Laozi enjoyed his family reunion in peace and seclusion. Li Tong became a general of the State of Zhao later on.

◎老子沛泽感怀图

Laozi responding to the social turmoil in Peize

老子在沛泽隐居数年后，宋国也发生内乱。烽烟中，老子看到田地长满蒿草，民不聊生，不禁大呼："天下无道，戎马生于郊""师生所处，荆棘生焉。大军之后，必有凶年"。老子决定离开沛泽前往秦国。

受国之垢，是谓社稷主；受国不祥，是谓天下王。（《老子》第七十八章）

Laozi enjoyed peace and seclusion for several years in Peize, and then Song went through its internal strife. In the smoke and fire, Laozi seemed to see the fields covered with weeds, and ordinary people could not survive. Laozi lamented,

"When the society is in chaos, the horses are enlisted in the war" "Where armies have been stationed, thorns and brambles grow. After a great war, harsh years of famine are sure to follow". Laozi hence decided to leave Peize for the State of Qin.

◎老子西行图
Laozi traveling west

　　老子此次西行骑的是青牛。青牛背宽，骑在上面稳当且舒服。青牛不但能陆行，还能涉水过河。经过千里跋涉，老子已远远望见通往秦国的必经关口——函谷关。

我有三宝，持而保之。一曰慈，二曰俭，三曰不敢为天下先。（《老子》第六十七章）

Laozi traveled to the west on a black ox. The black ox had so broad a back that it was comfortable to ride on. The black ox could travel both on land and in water. After many miles of travel, Laozi finally saw Hangu Pass to Qin in the distance.

◎老子、尹喜函谷关相见图
Laozi meeting Yin Xi in Hangu Pass

　　在函谷关，老子见到了老朋友关令尹喜。尹喜曾和老子同朝为官，他常到守藏室内向老子请教学问，被老子视为知音。尹喜善观天象，这天，尹喜望见紫气东来，便出关口相迎，即见老子到来。二人相见，交谈甚欢。尹喜对老子提出的政治、人生、道德感悟很感兴趣，建议老子把它们写下来传给后世。老子见尹喜要求强烈，盛情难却，便慨然应允。

孔德之容，惟道是从。（《老子》第二十一章）

In Hangu Pass, Laozi met his friend Yin Xi. Yin Xi had been an official serving the same royal family as Laozi did. Yin Xi often consulted Laozi when Laozi was working in the library. They were friends keenly appreciative of each other's talents. Yin Xi was good at interpreting the astronomical signs. He read a good sign that day and then, he went out of the pass to meet Laozi. The two talked with laughter bursting out from time to time. Yin Xi showed a strong interest in Laozi's ideas about politics, life and moral virtues, and suggested that Laozi write them down and pass down to future generations. Laozi found it hard to decline Yin Xi's earnest request and gladly accepted his advice.

◎老子函谷关著经图
Laozi writing Daode Jing in Hangu Pass

合抱之木，生于毫末；九层之台，起于累土；千里之行，始于足下。（《老子》第六十四章）

老子在函谷关住了下来。几十年来，老师商容、常枞的教诲，自己遍阅古籍的感悟，人生阅历的思索，时事风云的变化，与天人万物之启发……皆幻化为《老子》的名句书写于竹简之上。老子书写着，畅述着，一部流传千古的名著在这里诞生了。

Laozi settled down in Hangu Pass to write. He recalled the instruction of his masters Shang Rong and Chang Cong, the revelation from reading classical literature, and the experience gained from the ups and downs in life. Laozi turned them into memorable quotes on bamboo slips. Under his brush, an immortal masterpiece was born.

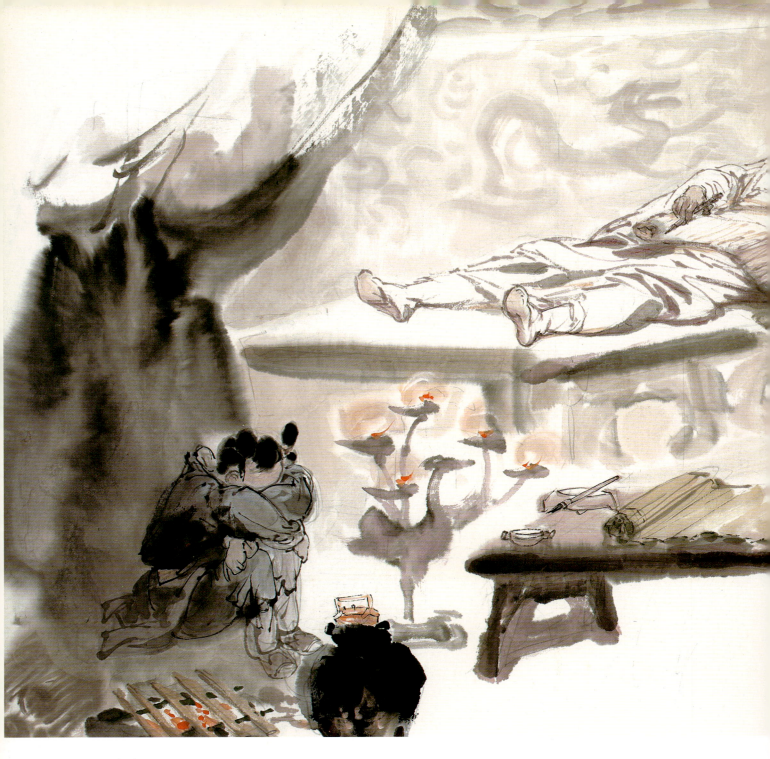

◎尹喜读经图

Yin Xi being the first reader

　　老子著经，尹喜先睹为快。他展开竹简，看到："道可道，非常道；名可名，非常名。无，名天地之始；有，名万物之母……"老子破天荒提出"道"这个概念，作为自己哲学思想体系的核心。老子的"道"具有一种对宇宙人生的独到解析和深刻感悟。这种对自然和自然规律的敬畏与尊重，构成了老子哲学思想的基石。"道"论是中国哲学史上第一个系统的宇宙论，对后世的哲学产生了重大而深远的影响。尹喜既惊喜又钦佩，决心要跟随老子，弃官问道。

道可道，非常道；名可名，非常名。（《老子》第一章）

Laozi immersed himself in writing, and Yin Xi immersed himself in an anxious reading. He unfolded the bamboo slips and read, "A discussable Tao is not an eternal Tao; a definable name is not an eternal name; the universe starts with no names, but when naming starts, that is the origin of everything." Laozi put forward for the first time in human history the concept of Tao, and set it in the center of his philosophy. Tao proposed by Laozi showed his profound understanding about universe and life. The respect for nature and its rules constituted the cornerstone of Laozi's philosophical thinking. Tao was the first systematic discussion about the universe in the history of philosophy in China, exerting a great impact upon philosophical schools in later generations. Yin Xi was both surprised and awed, and decided to leave his office and study under Laozi.

◎老子悟道图

Laozi attaining enlightenment

　　尹喜向老子请教什么是"道"的核心精神。老子说："人法地，地法天，天法道，道法自然。"意思是说，人以地为法，地以天为法，天以道为法，道以自然本性为法。人类生活与天地存在是一体的。人类要平安生存，唯有天安、地安，人类才能长安。"道"的深层意蕴是"安"。"安平泰"是道家文化的核心精神。

人法地，地法天，天法道，道法自然。（《老子》第二十五章）

Yin Xi asked Laozi what the essence of Tao was. Laozi explained to him, "Man follows the ways of the Earth; the Earth follows the ways of Heaven; Heaven follows the ways of Tao; Tao follows its own ways." The human being, the Earth and Heaven are in one unity. Only when the Earth and Heaven are at ease, can human beings keep tranquil. The meaning underlying Tao is resting peacefully. Peace is the essence of Taoism.

◎老子治大国若烹小鲜图
Governing a big country is as delicate as frying a small fish

　　老子在函谷关写出了五千言的《老子》（也称《道德经》）。《老子》书中包含大量的朴素辩证法观点，如"反者道之动""祸兮福之所倚，福兮祸之所伏"。老子以"道"作为其思想核心，所以他所创立的学派被称为"道家"，"合于道"为道家学者所追求的终极目标。《老子》中的许多经典名句，如"上善若水""治大国若烹小鲜"等被传诵至今，成为人们日常生活和社会生活中的座右铭。

治大国，若烹小鲜。（《老子》第六十章）

In Hangu Pass Laozi wrote the 5000-word *Laozi* (now it is also called *Daode Jing*). There are a lot of simple dialectical views in *Laozi*, for instance, "The movement of the Tao proceeds by contraries" "Good fortune leans on bad fortune and bad fortune could rest on good fortune". Laozi had Tao as his essence of thinking, and hence the school he established is called "Taoism". "Complying with nature" is the ultimate pursuit of Taoists. There are many quotable quotes in *Laozi*, such as "The great virtue is like water" "Governing a big country is as delicate as frying a small fish". Many people treat them as mottos to guide their life.

◎老子隐居扶风图

Laozi living in seclusion in Fufeng

老子到达秦国后，遍游名山大川，隐居于扶风、周至（今陕西省扶风县、周至县）一带讲学。由于学识高深，宽以待人，老子深受当地百姓爱戴。老子曾在槐里（在今陕西省周至县）讲学，去世后，那里的百姓怀念他，将他葬于槐里。在周至，至今还留有当年老子与弟子共同植下的银杏古树，此树虽逾两千余年，仍枝繁叶茂。

功遂身退，天之道也。（《老子》第九章）

In Qin, Laozi visited all the famous mountains and rivers, and then stayed undisturbed in Fufeng and Zhouzhi (now in Shaanxi Province), giving lectures. Laozi had great learning and kindness, and local people loved and respected him. Laozi once gave lectures in Huaili (now in Zhouzhi). When he passed away, people there buried him. The ginkgo tree Laozi and his disciples planted in Zhouzhi has survived more than 2000 years and is still flourishing.

◎老子道德千古图
The immortal Laozi

　　老子的道家学说，以经验实例论证了恒常之道的特征，教给人们在日常生活中认识事物，保持平安优胜、获得和谐幸福的方法。老子学说揭示了深刻博大的宇宙法则，极大提升了传统文化的理论思辨性，在中华文化的历史长河里，闪耀着璀璨的光芒。《老子》也被译成多种文字介绍到世界各地，对世界哲学体系的建立产生了深远的影响。

执古之道，以御今之有。能知古始，是谓道纪。（《老子》第十四章）

Laozi's Taoism tended to illustrate a profound idea with a simple example, teaching the ordinary people the way to get to know things in daily life and the way to live a harmonious and happy life. Laozi's teaching revealed the broad and profound truth about the universe, and enhanced the critical thinking in our traditional culture, shining brightly in the history of Chinese culture. *Laozi* has been translated into many languages and has exerted a great impact upon the world philosophy.

郭德福在河南鹿邑老子故居地
Guo Defu's field trip in Laozi's former residence, Luyi, Henan Province

作者手记

窗外松涛依旧。从 2012 年至今，我用三年做了一个艺术之梦——穿过神秘喧嚣的历史风尘，追寻生活中真实的老子，创作完成了《老子画传》。

我走出书房，走出画室，迈开双脚直赴河南鹿邑，叩开老子故宅的家门。我漫步在老子童年牧牛的野坡，瞻仰老子母亲益寿氏的墓地，重走青年老子从鹿邑远行周都洛邑的北漂之路，沿途感悟千里求学对青年老子的深刻影响，寻找老子悟『道』的文化源头与哲学基础。

我为在洛阳市第二十四中学校园内寻到老子故居地，并发现老子故宅前的瀍河而兴奋；为在菜市场找到的『孔子适周问礼于老子』古碑而激动不已。我上邙山，走黄河，经过几番探寻考证，我又有了一连串的意外收获，基本确定了馆藏史老子在洛邑近 30 年生活的范围和诸多生活细节。

我又从老子隐居地江苏沛县出发，探访老子的著经之地——河南函谷关，沿途的风土人情、历史遗迹，都为我描绘老子参悟风云世事、百态人生、乾坤宇宙、自然奥秘的智者形象增添了生活依据。

几番千里之行，几番史实探秘，几番沿途采风，生活中老子的喜、怒、哀、乐，老子的为人、为夫、为父、为师、为友、为官，都渐渐呈现于我的脑海中。在绘画中，我将自己保持在忆写的艺术状态中，不是杜撰，而像是与老子一起回忆他的人生，力求真实自然地塑造人物形象。为了增强艺术感染力，我吸收了法国印象派和当代绘画艺术的元素，追求呈现老子悟『道』过程中亦真亦幻、难以言说的文化风韵。

在撰写文稿时，我吸收了司马迁著《史记》所采用的历史真实、逻辑真实与艺术真实相融合的方法，力求通俗，希望通过这本画传能让更多的读者走近生活中真实的老子。

推窗望去，天云浩浩，我感到释然，我已经初步完成自己生命中要承担的使命……用半生的艺术积累、十三年的光阴，先后完成了《孔子画传》《老子画传》。我还要画下去，继续画生活中的孔子、老子，也还要继续走下去，走近历史的真实，走近生活的真实……

郭德福
甲午年孟冬

郭德福在河南洛阳寻访"孔子适周问礼于老子"古碑
Guo Defu's at the stone tablet where Confucius consulted Laozi

The Artist's Words

From my window I heard the soughing of the wind in the pines. Since 2012, I've been aspiring to travel back into the misty and dusty history so that I could finish my creating of *Laozi*.

I walked out of my studio, and left for Laozi's former residence in Luyi city, Henan Province. I visited the hill where Laozi's cattle grazed and the tomb where his mother was buried. I walked on the same trail the young Laozi walked from Luyi, his hometown, to Luoyi, the capital of Zhou. I tried to understand in my visit how this journey had impacted the young Laozi's life, and his philosophical thinking about life and universe.

In Luoyang (in ancient times known Luoyi, the capital of Zhou), I was so thrilled to be able to locate Laozi's residence in a middle school, and the Chanhe River in front of his residence. I continued my search, and I found in the market the stone tablet mark the spot where Confucius had consulted Laozi. On Mangshan Mountain, I had unexpected discoveries after some exploration. All this constitute a clear picture about the librarian Laozi who lived for 30 years in Luoyi. I then set out from Peixian in Jiangsu Province, where Laozi sought seclusion, to visit Hangu Pass in Henan Province. The sceneries and customs I saw along the way all contributed to my painting of Laozi, the sage who saw through the ups and downs of life, the mysteries of the universe.

My field trips covering thousands of *li* paid off. I could see a real Laozi as if Laozi himself was walking with me through his life: Laozi with all his emotions and Laozi as a man, husband, father, master, friend, and official. When painting, I tried to keep as faithfully as possible what I felt about Laozi while I was sketching. To demonstrate the indefinable revelation process Laozi got about Tao, I weaved some Impressionist elements and contemporary artistic expression into my painting in order to enhance the artistic appeal.

When writing, I adopted a writing style that is unique to *Records of the Historian*, combining history and logic, art and reality, making this book easy to read without losing its charm. I hope that reading this book will bring Laozi closer to the readers.

I felt so relieved seeing the clouds outside of my window. I have accomplished what I was meant to do. With all my ink painting skills and thirteen years time, I completed *Confucius* and *Laozi*. I will continue my artistic pursuit to portray Confucius and Laozi, walking closer to the history, closer to the truth…

Guo Defu
November 2014

后记

中国国家主席习近平在谈及中华文化时，深刻地指出："中华优秀传统文化已经成为中华民族的基因，植根在中国人内心，潜移默化影响着中国人的思想方式和行为方式。"厚重、灿烂的中华传统文化，如何借由一种生动、直观、亲切的方式走进读者，尤其是海外读者的阅读视野中，一直是文化界关注、思索的问题。当《诸子百家国风画传》丛书带着"传承、创新、中国风"的鲜明印迹从上海出发，正是希望由此探索向世界传播、普及中国优秀传统文化的新方式和新渠道。

上海，作为国际文化大都市，通过源源不断地推出文化交流精品，成为海外读者了解中国、感受中国的一扇精彩窗口。发源于上海的连环画艺术，则以其浓郁、独特的中国韵味深受国内外读者的欢迎。两年前，以传承、振兴中国连环画艺术为主旨的上海海派连环画中心甫一成立，即在上海市政府新闻办的指导、创意下，联合发起策划一套以国风连环画为载体、契合"读图时代"特点的《诸子百家国风画传》丛书，并得到了

国务院新闻办公室、中共上海市委宣传部的大力支持，以及山东、河南省政府新闻办和相关诸子故里的密切协作。

尤为可贵的是，国内著名国画家郭德福、李维定、赵明钧、邵家声、忻秉勇为淋漓再现智者先贤而实地采风，遍览典籍、泼墨挥毫，精益求精，创作出让人耳目一新、形神兼备的诸子数易其稿，精益求精，创作出让人耳目一新、形神兼备的诸子形象。画传不仅选取诸子生平中最具典型意义的事件，还注意表现鲜有人关注的诸子日常生活。画传想让读者感知的不只是存在于文献、传说里的古之圣贤，更是身边熟悉亲切、可以答疑解惑的智者。

我们衷心希望，这套充满哲理智慧与中国艺术美质的丛书能够成为连接当代与中华传统的文化桥梁，希望中华文化的寻源之旅能让每一个中国人寻回精神归属，也让海外读者从另一蹊径了解中国文化之美。

《诸子百家国风画传》丛书编委会
二〇一四年九月

Afterword

President Xi Jinping made an insightful comment in his talking about Chinese culture, "The excellent traditional Chinese culture has become our genes deeply rooted in our heart, entered into and colored our patterns in thinking and behaving." How the rich and brilliant Chinese culture could be presented in a vivid, visual and approachable form to the readers, especially overseas readers, has always been the concern of the cultural circle. When *The Pictorial Biographies of Great Thinkers* series with its distinguishing features of "inheritance, originality, and Chinese style" is setting sail from Shanghai, it is hoped to be a new means and a new channel explored for spreading, popularizing the excellent Chinese culture.

As an international cultural metropolis, Shanghai has created continuously first-class cultural exchange project and become a window through which overseas readers get to know and understand China. The comic book painting art originated in Shanghai has always been well accepted by readers home and abroad for its rich and unique Chinese style. Two years ago, not long after Shanghai Comic Book Center established to inherit and revive the comic painting art, under the guidance of Information Office of Shanghai Municipality, the Center created a series of comic book — *The Pictorial Biographies of Great Thinkers* to appeal to the "visual era". This innovative project is supported by The State Council Information Office and Publicity Ministry of Shanghai Municipal committee of CPC, and this project is also a close cooperation between Information Office of Shandong Provincial People's Government, Information Office of Henan Provincial People's Government and Confucius hometown.

What made this series particularly valuable is the research work the artists did. To represent thoroughly and faithfully the great thinkers, Mr. Guo Defu, Mr. Zhao Mingjun, Mr. Shao Jiasheng and Mr. Xin Bingyong, not only read extensively the classics but also conducted field work. They tried different means of expression and revised numerous times for a better unity of appearance and spirit of the thinkers. The episodes in the pictorial biographies reveal both the milestone events great thinkers experienced and their daily life that usually went unnoticed. The great thinkers in the pictorial biographies are no longer legendary figure in the literature, but amiable saints we can approach with our problems for a solution.

We sincerely hope that this series rich in philosophical wisdom and Chinese aestheticism could bridge the contemporary China and its traditional culture. We also hope that the exploration of Chinese culture will give every Chinese a sense of spiritual belonging, and provide an alternative for overseas readers to get to know the beauty of Chinese culture.

Editing Committee of *The Pictorial Biographies of Great Thinkers*
September 2014